How I *Forgave* My Molester

I can do everything through him who gives me strength.

Philippians 4:13

MELINDA TODD

Author of Trailing After God

Disclaimer:

The material in this book is the author's sole opinions and experiences. It is not medical advice. The author is not a doctor, counselor or expert. These materials are for educational purposes only and should be used with discretion. The author is not liable or responsible with respect to any loss or damage caused by use of this information. Please do not use this information if you do not choose to be bound by the above.

Note from the author

To protect identities, some names may have been changed. I have completely forgiven "Uncle Max" and it would not be beneficial to either of us if I were to release his true identity. I cannot say with one side of my mouth that I have forgiven and then with the other attack and ruin his life. Those involved know who they are. The true message is Christ and the freedom He offers each of us.

Published by Melinda Todd
http://melindatodd.com

Printed in the United States of America

ISBN - 978-0-61-547746-6

Acknowledgments

I'd like to thank Christian Author, Michelle Sutton for believing in my story and giving me the courage to pursue publishing. Thank you for seeing how this booklet can help hurting women who have been abused, recover and heal. I thank my mom for encouraging me to share my story. Thanks to my sweet husband who has stuck by me through some really tough times and continues to stand by my side. Thanks to my friend Margaret for giving me a new tape to play and for always praying for me!

This book is dedicated to my precious friend, a survivor like me. I don't know you but I pray this book helps you take back what once was lost and allows you to look forward to a bright future that isn't overshadowed by your past. May you find the healing love of God while you take this journey. You're not alone as you traverse down this new path. You can be healed and move beyond the abuse.

Prologue

Lost Innocence

Her big blue eyes pooled with tears as she looked up at him. She heard his angry words but didn't understand the meanness she could sense in his voice and actions. Her lower lip trembled while tears formed little rivers down her freckled cheeks.

"I want mommy," she whispered. "Where's mommy?" She sniffed back the snot that was dribbling from her little nose, rubbing her face with her little girl hands.

"You will do what I say!" he screamed, raising the piece of wood he gripped in his hand. "You do what I say, Mel, or I will beat you with this stick."

She cowered at the idea of being struck with the long piece of wood. She began to twirl her brown curls around her finger, sucking her thumb like she always did when she was upset. Confusion struck her four year old mind.

Uncle Max is supposed to play with me while Mom and Daddy are gone, isn't he? He's always nice, even when he tickles me until I cry.

Mommy, save me. Daddy, please come home. Something's wrong. Something's wrong with Uncle Max. He wants to hurt me. How can he hurt me? Doesn't he love me? He's supposed to love me.

That night changed her life in unimaginable ways – her innocence stolen forever, pieces of her tender heart permanently burnt and scattered like ashes among the sea.

1

You keep track of all my sorrows.
You have collected all my tears in your bottle.
You have recorded each one in your book.

Psalm 56:8

My innocence was lost on that fateful night. Broken and charred, I had to learn to become a new child. I wish I could say that what you just read is all I remember of this episode, but it's not. I only remember a little bit more detail and thankfully nothing more.

I'm not certain if I was only molested once, but circumstances recently led me to believe that it was not the only time this took place.

My memories about telling my mom what happened are vague. I may have told her more than once. I recall my step-sister forcing me to tell. She dragged me into the living room.

"Tell her what happened," she instructed.

I remember my mom asking me where Uncle Max had touched me. I couldn't bring myself to speak the words. I just pointed to the place I knew he shouldn't have touched. I was ashamed. I knew Uncle Max was going to get into trouble and I felt bad for him. I didn't understand all that had taken place, but I knew it felt *wrong*.

I don't know what my mom said to Uncle Max or if he got in trouble. It was never discussed again, and Uncle Max was still a part of our life. He came to family gatherings, and visited often. My parents never spoke of it with me, so I never brought it up.

I felt betrayed. The people who were supposed to love me didn't seem to care that someone who was also supposed to love me had hurt me.

I knew in my little girl mind that Uncle Max should have been in big trouble. I mean, I got in trouble for stealing chocolate-covered raisins from the crystal dish with the lid that clinked if I accidentally brushed it against the base - that lid gave me away every time - or when I scooped peanut butter out of the jar with my fingers and lied about it.

But Uncle Max didn't get in trouble at all. It was confusing, and I learned at a juvenile age that some people never get into trouble for doing awful things.

I would discover years later the reason Uncle Max was not charged or removed from my life was due to advice my mom received from her own mother. Grandma said maybe if everyone pretended nothing had happened and they didn't make a big deal about it, maybe it wouldn't bother me.

Unfortunately, neither of them could know the message it actually sent me was that I wasn't important and that no one loved me enough to protect me. Instead of shielding me, the innocent child, they protected the abuser.

This shattered any chance of a healthy self-esteem. I beat myself up with unhealthy thoughts.

Melinda Todd

Why wasn't I enough? Why wasn't I important enough to anyone? Why me?

I was doing a lot of asking "why" without getting any answers.

I remember one especially bad day when I was eleven. Things were falling apart at home, and my parents were separated. I was living with my dad, and he had people constantly moving in and out of our house.

On that particular day as I strolled up the pathway to our house after school, my heart hurt so bad. I decided I wasn't going to let the pain get to me anymore.

"I'm not real, I am a robot," I chanted, "I have no feelings, I am a robot. I am a robot. I am a robot." I repeated this to my internal self for days and it seemed to work. I began to compartmentalize anything that could possibly draw pain out of me. If it hurt or had potential to hurt, I put it into my robot place and I left it there to die.

I was always so good at hiding my feelings. If I pretended to be happy then everyone else seemed happy. Some of us are born people-pleasers, and I was no exception to the rule. Better to remain silent than hurt someone, right?

During elementary school I was the only girl among all the cousins, and I was the "good one." I got the good grades. I won the spelling bees, and I made the right choices - or so I let them believe. Everyone had high expectations of me, and I was busy doing my best to live up to those expectations.

Little did anyone know, I was dying behind my self-made façade. The lies I was living in were making me lonely. I had stuffed everything: the abuse by my uncle, the divorce, moving far away from friends, and losing the life I had known.

2

~ It is for freedom that Christ has set us free.
Stand firm, then, and do not let yourselves be
burdened again by a yoke of slavery.
Galatians 5:1 ~

"How can you stand to be in the same house as *him*?" My step-sister asked me when she came to visit during spring break of my freshman year. I was living with my dad again, and she and I were in my bedroom talking. It took a while for her words to finally register with me.

"What?" Our eyes made contact. I knew she was referring to how often Uncle Max came over to my dad's to visit.

"How can you be around *Uncle Max*? Why does your mom let him anywhere near you?" she questioned. "My mom doesn't want *me* anywhere near him and honestly, I hate being around him after what he did to us!" My stepsister smoothed the wrinkles in the comforter as she spoke.

"And *why* does *Dad* let him come here?" she asked in a whisper.

"You mean he did *that* to you too?" I asked, feeling shocked. I took a deep breath while allowing her acknowledgment to sink in. If he did to her what he did to me, then maybe he had touched other girls. I shuddered at the thought.

How many girls were there? Someone should have done something a long time ago.

"I'm sorry," I told her. "I didn't know it happened to you too." We kept talking, and things became a little clearer. But at the same time, I felt more confused than ever.

The revelation that my step-sister had been abused just like me would haunt me for the next year-and-a-half. At some point, I convinced myself that I'd never had that conversation with my step-sister.

I began telling myself that maybe the reason everyone acted like nothing happened was because I was crazy. Maybe it never really did happen.

In my mind, it seemed easier to pretend the abuse had never occurred than to have to focus on it and deal with it. It appeared to work for the rest of the family, so why not for me?

But adding craziness to my robot façade didn't work. In fact, it actually made it much worse. Thinking I was crazy and that I had only imagined something so horrible was unhealthy for me. Buying that kind of lie only damaged my psyche even further.

I became one of those girls that sought male attention and, while I wasn't promiscuous, I always had a boyfriend. It was hard for me to believe that a decent man would want me, so I settled for boys with whom I had no business being around. After all, I was tarnished, stained, impure, and dirty. Who would want me for keeps?

One afternoon when I felt like cracking apart, I sat down and wrote my mom a letter.

Melinda Todd

"Dear Mom,

I feel like I am crazy. I want to believe that Uncle Max didn't sexually abuse me as a child but I know deep down, he did. I know I told you. It happened, didn't it? Why did nothing happen to him? Why does everyone pretend everything is fine when there is a child molester among us? I can't keep living a lie. I'm not okay. What happened to me is not okay. What if he abuses the other little girls in our family? I couldn't live with myself if he has."

Of course, then my mother confirmed what I knew in my heart to be true, and she got me into counseling. Finally, the secret monster had been let out of the dark closet and there was no putting it back.

However, true to my robot personality I played the part of being "healed" and convinced my mom after two sessions that I was fine and no longer needed to go. Ending my counseling sessions was not the smartest move on my part, but at age sixteen I wasn't ready. I didn't want to have this problem and I didn't want to talk about it with some stranger.

While I was going through that short amount of counseling, I had a boyfriend who made me feel special, important and - best of all - loved. He listened to the horror of my past and loved me anyway. When I cried over my loss of purity, he reassured me I was perfect.

How I Forgave My Molester

3

~ *"I tell you the truth, if you have faith as small as a mustard seed, you can say to this mountain, 'Move from here to there' and it will move.*
Nothing will be impossible for you."
Matthew 17:20 ~

As it turned out, my sixteen year-old high school sweetheart would later become my husband and my best friend. By nineteen, I was married and had my first child, a son. When I looked into his tiny, perfect little face, all I could think was how I would feel like dying if anyone ever put their hands on this tiny person in the way Uncle Max put his hands on me.

How am I going to protect this child? How do I know who to trust? If anyone ever lays a hand on you, I will kill them.

The mama bear in me couldn't fathom the explosion that would take place in my brain and heart if I ever found out someone had touched one of my babies inappropriately.

*Why wasn't that **their** response? Why didn't my dad want to kill him? My husband would end up in jail if anyone touched his boy. So would I.*

15

I proceeded to go through a time in my marriage when the idea of anything sexually intimate actually repulsed me. So much so, that I would feel physically ill at the slightest idea of sex. My husband tried to understand, but my marriage was rocky for a while, not because my husband wasn't kind to me at that time, but because he couldn't help feeling rejected.

Through a lot of prayers, the Lord led me through those slow, tough days. I began to realize that maybe the reason the abuse happened to me was because He was going to use my experience to help others. That knowledge helped give me some peace in my heart, and God showed me that being intimate with my husband was not sinful, dirty, or scary.

When my son reached the age I remembered being when I was abused, it was like a switch had been flipped. By this time I had worked through a lot of ill feelings and ideas I had about sex. But I suddenly needed more answers. And I was determined to get them.

In order to get my answers and finally confront the monster living in my heart, I went straight to the source. Writing my mother a letter had helped me begin to heal, so I wrote Uncle Max a letter, and I poured my heart into it. I didn't hold anything back. If he was going to know how he had affected my life, then he needed to hear every bit of it. The boldness of my letter brought me quite a bit of freedom, though it didn't all happen overnight.

"Dear Uncle Max:

How could you? Why did you take my innocence? What did I do to deserve this? Do you know that you changed me forever? You took something precious from me. You changed who I am in my

Melinda Todd

marriage and with my husband... You've been at every family function, forcing me to face you and pretend everything was fine. Why was our whole family so comfortable with a child molester sitting among us? Why wasn't anyone angry enough with you to want to wring your neck?... "

How I Forgave My Molester

4

~ Be kind and compassionate to one another,

forgiving each other,

just as in Christ God forgave you.

Ephesians 4:32 ~

To my utter amazement, Uncle Max wrote back. Not only did he admit what he had done, he shared with me how his guilt had impacted his life.

Dear Mel:

"I did do those horrible things and I will never forgive myself... Those same things were done to me by my brother's friend when I was little and I continued the abuse... I'm so sorry... I have lived with my guilt... Drug abuse... Suicide attempts... I wish I could take it back. I wish I could change what happened... I'm so sorry... I know you and God can't forgive me... I will go to hell for what I have done... I tried to walk with the Lord at one time but it was no use... There is no escaping what I have done... Matthew 18:6 But if anyone causes one of these little ones who believe in me to sin, it would be better for him to have a large millstone hung around his neck and to be drowned in the depths of the sea... I am so sorry for the damage I have done to your life... So sorry, I can never express it enough...."

It's amazing how an apology - even for something so horrific - can move the heart closer to healing. Maybe because I grew up with Uncle Max as a part of my life, and there was a relationship - as odd, awkward and dysfunctional as it was – it made it easier to accept and believe his apology.

Years later I was able to speak to Uncle Max face-to-face about this. I have forgiven him in person, not just through a letter. I have told him there is forgiveness through Jesus.

Uncle Max's guilt for a sin so loathsome has made his life hopeless and despairing. I have watched that guilt traipse across his life, destroying everything that comes across his path. In his own eyes - and likely most of the human world - he has performed the one unforgivable sin. I have witnessed the self-destruction of his life, firsthand.

While his acts turn the human flesh and mind, the truth is that Christ's blood covers them all, not just the minor ones we agree with but even the scandalous and revolting sins that tear people apart and ruin lives. It's a hard pill to swallow, isn't it?

I can't explain my feelings of forgiveness, other than to say I believe they are truly an act of God. Understanding the mercy, love, and forgiveness of Christ for my sinful heart, I could feel within me the longing to set Uncle Max free and forgive him.

I know some people believe forgiveness isn't about the perpetrator, but rather about the victim and helping the victim heal. But I found for myself that there was a part of me that wanted Uncle Max to feel my forgiveness and know God's love, mercy and complete forgiveness, too

20

Melinda Todd

Also, I now understand why my mom and grandma chose their path of silence. Perhaps my grandma hoped that it was something I'd made up or had seen on television, but I understand now she came from a time and place where these things were not talked about. It wasn't like things are today when everyone goes for the jugular when the truth comes out. I'm so glad we are changing how this is viewed and dealt with now. But back then this was a private matter and one just did not talk about such things openly. So, it was brushed under the rug.

This understanding led me to forgive my mom and family for the choices they made. They did what they thought was best and the rest of the family pretended that everything was fine because that's what I did.

My mom is now one of my best friends. We can talk about my abuse, and she knows God is at work in my life. Now I pray for my mom to be released from any guilt that she still lugs around with her. It's too heavy a burden and a potential trap for her walk with the Lord.

I don't know how God is going to continue to use me. I do know that one night while trying to get to sleep, I was told to write, to tell the hard stories, the ones that hurt me the most. Because my life can give others hope.

When I say I have hope, peace and freedom, what I mean by that is that I no longer feel a punch to the gut when I think about my past and the abuse. I can breathe easier. My memories aren't always lurking in the back of my mind, ready to jump out at me and shout, "***Boo***!" at any given moment.

I don't like what Uncle Max did, and he's not going to ever be my buddy or hang out with my kids, but I don't feel hatred for him any longer. I have a peace about the situation. Do the memories and feelings still creep up now and again? Yes, but I don't allow them to stay.

Before I found healing and forgiveness I would let the negative emotions take over my thoughts, seep into my life and poison my happy moments. Now I've learned to recognize it for what it is: A snare of the devil and a foothold that Satan will gladly take if given the chance.

Slowly but surely, I am learning that I have the ability to take my thoughts captive and stop the sewer seepage into my life. There's no place for it now. It's in the past. I can't change what happened, but I can change what comes of it. If I can help one woman move past this, then it will all be worth it.

5

How To Claim Your Healing

~ It is for freedom that Christ has set us free. Stand firm, then, and do not let yourselves be burdened again by a yoke of slavery.
Galatians 5:1 ~

I pray that this booklet and story gives you hope for peace. If my readers can find some measure of healing by reading my story, then that would be the best gift I could ever be presented with from my life and pain.

Not everyone will feel compelled to forgive his or her abuser, but this is what worked for me. I pray you will go on this journey with me and that you can claim victory!

God knows you can and He's going to be there celebrating with you when it happens. And so will I!

The value of forgiving will bless you and set you free from the bondage you have with your abuser and that is the ultimate goal. Take your power back. As long as you hold any feelings, other than forgiveness towards them, you give them control over your life. They've taken enough from you. Don't give them anymore!

The big question for me truly came down to trust, so I want to lovingly and gently ask you, my precious reader, are you ready to believe and trust that God is enough? That He and only He can truly set you completely free? His word says you are set free.

Galatians 5:1 says: It is for **freedom** that Christ has set us free. Stand firm, then, and do not let yourselves be burdened again by a yoke of slavery. *Do you see that?* For *freedom* we have been set *free*. It doesn't stop there, does it? No, it continues to say, "Do not let yourselves be burdened again by a **yoke of slavery**." *A yoke of slavery*!

The pain, trauma, and unforgiveness you are carrying around right now are a yoke of slavery. But they don't have to be. Honest. You can let them go and enjoy your life.

Take your pain to the foot of the cross. Leave it there once and for all. The blood that Jesus shed will cover it. It already has. Once you have left it, *don't come back for it*. **Trust Jesus to be enough. He is enough. He's it.**

Dear *Sweet, precious child of God*. Come closer. Can you hear Him whispering truth in your heart? You **can** be **healed**. You can be whole and pure again! There is complete redeeming power in the sacrificial blood of The lamb. You can take back your power. You can move forward. And you can have peace in your heart and in your life. Jesus has already set you free, now you need to claim it!

While you complete each step, please be in prayer and memorizing Scripture at the same time.

Pray Fervently

~ Your word I have treasured in my heart, that I may not sin against You.

Psalm 119:11 ~

I understand you may not believe in a loving God after what you have experienced but God knows **YOU** and desires for you to know Him. He already loves **you**. He's just waiting for you to come to Him. His word says all you need is faith the size of a mustard seed (Matthew 17:20). If you are ready for his healing power, all you have to do is tell Him you want Him in your life and He will take care of the rest.

Prayer is a very important step in your healing process. You don't have to speak eloquently to God, just be honest. Tell Him you hurt and you're angry. Tell Him you feel let down, unprotected, unloved, dirty, broken, discarded, and whatever else comes to mind. You can't surprise God. He's big enough to hear it all. Best of all, He's big enough to **heal** it all.

Get on your knees and start praying for the ability to forgive, to be healed, to be whole, and to finally be completely freed from this bondage. Pray until you start to feel released and then keep praying. Pray when you lie down, when you wake up, in the shower, while you drive, do the dishes, fold laundry, and anywhere else that you get a few minutes to do so. I know you want to do this on your own but you cannot. Receive the power from the Almighty. **Our perfect Heavenly Father is waiting with outstretched arms to carry you through this.** You're probably already in his arms and have been since you were victimized.

Prayer Examples:

"Lord, I come before you with a broken heart. I am laying my burdens down and asking for your help in healing. Pour your healing salve over the aching cracks in my heart. Your Word says that your burden is light but my burden has been so heavy, Lord. I pray for freedom and release from my heavy yoke. I ask for freedom and peace. In Jesus Name, Amen"

"Lord, your Word says you created me and you know the plans you have for me. You have plans to prosper me and to give me a hope and a future. Father, I am praying for hope and a future. I have felt alone and hopeless but today, I ask you to fill me with your hope and show me a new future, one without the pain and baggage of my abuse. In Jesus Name, Amen"

Reflection:

• List Bible verses you can insert your name into and use as a prayer:

Example: "Mel, Ask and it will be given to you; Mel, seek and you will find; Mel, knock and the door will be opened to you." Matthew 7:7

Melinda Todd

- What aches in your heart do you need to start praying over?

- Are there other people in your life that you can pray for?

- Do you have doubts or fears that you won't be able to win this battle?

How I Forgave My Molester

Melinda Todd

Tune Into Him – Media

~ Put away perversity from your mouth; keep corrupt talk far from your lips. Proverbs 4:24 ~

Tune into what you are putting into your mind via television, music, books, and internet. So much of secular music is extremely sexual and advocates affairs. Listening to Christian music and good, solid sermons can really help. I generally do not listen to anything but Christian music because I need my focus to stay positive. Focusing your thoughts on Christ is always a positive thing.

How often do you wake-up with a song in your head? For me, it's all the time. I hated waking up with sexually inappropriate lyrics running through my mind. I would catch myself singing the catchy tune and find my mind mulling over the story in the song. There was usually nothing uplifting to glean from the secular songs either. Now I wake up with praise and worship songs instead. When your heart is heavily burdened you need to surround yourself with positive messages.

I also advocate turning off the television for a while. Get quiet with the Lord. Hear His message instead of what the media is feeding you. Matthew 4:4 Jesus answered, "It is written: 'Man does not live on bread alone, but on every word that comes from the mouth of God." Feed yourself what is good, righteous and true and you will fight off the lies!

29

Read God's word first and foremost. Find Christian books that are uplifting and especially books that tell of survival and triumph. There are many amazing missionary stories that will inspire and encourage you. Christian fiction is a great genre to explore and includes romance, sci-fi, history, contemporary, fantasy, and many other styles of stories.

Reflections:

• Do you think media is important in your healing process?

• What media do you need to eliminate from your life even temporarily?

• Are there any television shows or movies that might be best to purge from your life? Why or why not?

Melinda Todd

• Will your family and friends be your support system while you wean from media?

• What will you do if your family and friends are not supportive?

• What steps can you take to introduce healthy books into your life?

• Where will you go to find clean Christian books to read?

• What Bible studies would you like to participate in?

How I Forgave My Molester

Melinda Todd

<u>**Memorize Scripture**</u>

~ And the words of the LORD are flawless, like silver refined in a furnace of clay, purified seven times. Psalm 12:6 ~

Getting into the Word of God and memorizing verses from the Bible will also help you with your healing. The Bible isn't just a to-do list; it's full of amazing affirmations for the abused. I've given you some verses that have helped me feel empowered, but you might want to choose your own. Just open a Bible and read until you find something that speaks to your heart.

Get some index cards because you are going to memorize some Scriptures. Start with one Scripture per week. Put that verse on cards in every room, anywhere you will regularly see them. Every time you see a Scripture card, I want you to say that Scripture **out loud**. Yes, **every single time**.

The more times you say a Bible verse out loud, the sooner you will commit it to memory. Speaking the words out loud will not only help you store them in your heart and mind, but Scripture has real power. Use it!

Get some of the window markers and write your verses on every mirror, the windows, the sliding glass door, and the fridge - anywhere you are sure to see it *every single day*.

You need to arm yourself with God's positive truths or risk losing the battle because Satan is going to try to keep you down. You

will have times where your thoughts are going to try run away with you. When that happens, you are going to tell yourself to **STOP**! Next, you need to pray for the ability to capture your thoughts. Then, recite your Scriptures out loud. This is where having memorized those Scriptures is going to be used extensively.

Please don't be naïve and skip this step. **It is paramount to complete your healing.**

Here are some suggested Scriptures to get you started:

* Therefore, if anyone is in Christ, he is a new creation; the old has gone, the new has come! 2 Corinthians 5:17

When we accept Christ's death on the cross as payment for all of our sins and invite him to be a part of our lives and our heart, we become a new creation. Not because of ourselves but because of what Christ has done for us.

* Be alert and of sober mind. Your enemy the devil prowls around like a roaring lion looking for someone to devour. 1 Peter 5:8

This verse is a good reminder that Satan is going to try to hamper our healing with negative thoughts.

* Be kind and compassionate to one another, forgiving each other, just as in Christ God forgave you. Ephesians 4:32

We've been forgiven for our sins. Even when it seems unfair, we are told to forgive others their sins against us. There will be days where forgiveness will seem too hard but God reminds us that Christ died for us and we didn't deserve it.

Melinda Todd

* "For I know the plans I have for you," declares the LORD, "plans to prosper you and not to harm you, plans to give you hope and a future." Jeremiah 29:11

This is my life verse. It is the one verse I cling to because of the promise God declares in it. We may not understand His plans right now but He's clear that He's got our lives covered. We have been given hope **and** a future!

* I can do everything through him who gives me strength. Philippians 4:13

We have been given the power to do even the hardest tasks. Forgiving an abuser is one of the hardest ordeals I have ever had to go through. I know the change in my heart is not from my own doing. My weak flesh does not have the ability to forgive Uncle Max without the power of the Holy Spirit.

* It is for freedom that Christ has set us free. Stand firm, then, and do not let yourselves be burdened again by a yoke of slavery. Galatians 5:1

Unforgiveness is a yoke of slavery. It's a heavy burden that follows you everywhere and affects everything you say, feel, and do. Christ has set us free and taken our heavy yoke upon Himself. You no longer have to haul around that festering bag of garbage from your abuse. Leave it at the foot of the cross and let God take care of it.

* Pray without ceasing. 1 Thessalonians 5:17

Prayer keeps us in touch with God. When we focus on God and prayer, it gives us the ability to release the tension from our life. If we get quiet with Him we will hear what He has to say to our hearts.

Memorize all of **Ephesians 6:10-18** because you are going to need the **full** armor of God to fight this fight. Trust me on this one.*

Reflection:

• Do you think God can work your situation for good? If so, explain how. If not, why do you feel that way?

• In what ways do you think Satan will try to rob you of your healing?

• What will you do when the negative thoughts come?

• Do you have a life verse? If not, pick a Bible verse that really speaks to your heart.

Melinda Todd

Claim It Out Loud

~ And the words of the LORD are flawless, like silver refined in a furnace of clay, purified seven times. Psalm 12:6 ~

The goal is to capture freedom in your life and grasp God's promises, so claim it out loud. Saying your Bible verses out loud has power. Saying, "I forgive you," out loud has amazing healing powers too. The more you say the Bible verse out loud, the more your mind will start to believe it. Claim it! It's yours to be had! **Claim it out loud in the name of Jesus! Amen!**

Please know, dear one, that forgiveness does not mean that you throw all caution to the wind. Forgiveness does not equal friendship. You can forgive and still avoid your abuser.

If you have been blaming yourself for what happened to you, claim forgiveness over yourself as well. You did nothing wrong. You are not responsible for the sickness of someone else's actions, no matter what.

Reflection:

• Why do you think speaking God's truth out loud is effective?

• Do you feel uncomfortable voicing your freedom in Christ? Explain why or why not.

Melinda Todd

<u>Seek Christian Counseling</u>

~ The way of a fool seems right to him, but a wise man listens to advice. Proverbs 12:15 ~

While you can do a lot of this work in your quiet times by yourself and with the Lord, please consider seeking out a Godly (faith-based) counselor to talk to. Maybe this should be the first step, but sometimes we have to start with some work on ourselves before we desire to seek help from an outsider.

Women, seek female counseling. I am not putting down the usefulness of male counselors, but if you have been abused sexually by a male or have abused yourself with sex and men, it is not wise or safe for you to seek a male counselor.

Don't settle for any counselor either. Pray for wisdom in choosing. Pray that God would bring the right counselor into your life. Don't be afraid to visit several but don't unload your story until you feel ready to trust the counselor you are sharing with and listen to their advice.

If you don't know how to find a Christian counselor, call your pastor who will know where to direct you or at least how to help you search for the right one. If you are not brave enough to do this yourself, ask a trusted friend to help. You can email me if you want. I can't give you counseling, but I can pray for you and I will make phone calls for you if I need to. There is a contact form on my blog at http://melindatodd.com to contact me.

Reflections:

• List trustworthy people you can call when you are struggling.

• Do you feel safe seeking a counselor? Why or why not?

• Is there a support group in your area for sexual abuse survivors?

• What would you like to find in a counselor?

• What are some traits (often found in a trusted friend) that you would like to look for in a counselor?

• Are you comfortable talking to your pastor or someone from your own church?

Melinda Todd

<u>Write</u>

~ *Hold on to instruction, do not let it go; guard it well,*
for it is your life. Proverbs 4:13 ~

One thing you can do to claim your freedom from the abuse you experienced is to write a letter. I won't advocate writing a letter that you actually mail to your abuser. The outcome of my letter is not the norm. Having the molester further deny their actions may cause even further damage to your broken heart and mind. I will tell you to write a letter you will never send. Feel free to let your abuser have it. Hold nothing back. Get angry. Get real. Get down in the dirty trenches and beat your abuser down with your words. Take your power back. You have the right to fight for yourself.

I don't believe the saying, "Fight for yourself because no one else will" because Christ will. **He did. He has already won the battle,** so you can be whole.

Once you finish venting in letter form, decide what you want to do with the letter. Will you burn it? Bury it in the backyard? Have your spouse read it? Send it. If you choose to send the letter, please pray about the outcome. You can send it anonymously or without a return address on it. Write as many letters as you need until you have said all you need to say. One letter may not be enough.

Another option is to journal how you feel about what happened.

41

You can explore your feelings about anyone else who was involved in the situation, whether through neglect, denial, blame, etc. Don't let your letter writing end with the abuser. Write letters to anyone whom you need to direct your feelings. I have even written letters to God. Write until you have nothing more to say.

• How did sexual abuse affect your life?

• List some feelings that come up when you think about your abuse?

• Who do you need to write letters to? Who was involved in the abuse?

• Are there people you need to forgive to start healing?

- Is there anyone in your life that will resist your healing?

- If someone resists your healing and the process, how can you respond to that person?

- Will you allow another person to hinder your progress?

- If you received a response to your letter from your abuser, what would be the worst response you could receive?

- What would be the best response?

• Are you prepared emotionally to deal with a negative response or denial from your abuser?

• If your abuser apologized would you accept their apology?

Melinda Todd

Provided is a list of many of the items that have assisted my healing process. Some were recommended to me by other abuse survivors.

Books/Studies:

The Bondage Breaker by Neil T. Anderson

Believing God by Beth Moore

The Mom I Want To Be by T. Suzanna Eller

The Wounded Heart (Hope For Adult Victims Of Childhood Sexual Abuse) by Dan B. Allender

Divine by Karen Kingsbury (fiction)

Music:

Beauty Will Rise by Steven Curtis Chapman. This song will bless your socks off while you fight this good fight!

Cry Out To Jesus by Third Day

Held by Natalie Grant

In Better Hands Now by Natalie Grant

Stronger by Mandisa

There Will Be A Day by Jeremy Camp

Healing Hand of God by Jeremy Camp

Open The Eyes Of My Heart Lord by Mercy Me

Your Love by Brandon Heath

What Love Really Means by JJ Heller

Voice Of Truth by Casting Crowns

You Are More by Tenth Avenue North

7 x 70 by Chris August

I Am New Jason Gray

Melinda Todd

 * I have provided the memory verses in the next few pages with a place for you to journal. Read the verses and decide how you can use them in your life.

Be kind and compassionate to one another, forgiving each other, just as in Christ God forgave you. Ephesians 4:32

For I know the plans I have for you," declares the LORD, "plans to prosper you and not to harm you, plans to give you hope and a future. Jeremiah

I can do everything through him who gives me strength.
Philippians 4:13

Therefore, if anyone is in Christ, he is a new creation; the old has gone, the new has come! 2 Corinthians 5:17

It is for freedom that Christ has set us free. Stand firm, then, and do not let yourselves be burdened again by a yoke of slavery. Galatians 5:1

Pray without ceasing.

1 Thessalonians 5:17

Finally, brothers and sisters, whatever is true, whatever is noble, whatever is right, whatever is pure, whatever is lovely, whatever is admirable—if anything is excellent or praiseworthy—think about such things. Philippians 4:8

48

Melinda Todd

The Armor of God

Finally, be strong in the Lord and in his mighty power. [11] Put on the full armor of God, so that you can take your stand against the devil's schemes. [12] For our struggle is not against flesh and blood, but against the rulers, against the authorities, against the powers of this dark world and against the spiritual forces of evil in the heavenly realms. [13] Therefore put on the full armor of God, so that when the day of evil comes, you may be able to stand your ground, and after you have done everything, to stand. [14] Stand firm then, with the belt of truth buckled around your waist, with the breastplate of righteousness in place, [15] and with your feet fitted with the readiness that comes from the gospel of peace. [16] In addition to all this, take up the shield of faith, with which you can extinguish all the flaming arrows of the evil one. [17] Take the helmet of salvation and the sword of the Spirit, which is the Word of God.

[18] And pray in the Spirit on all occasions with all kinds of prayers and requests. With this in mind, be alert and always keep on praying for all the Lord's people.
Ephesians 6:10-18

How I Forgave My Molester

www.ingramcontent.com/pod-product-compliance
Lightning Source LLC
Chambersburg PA
CBHW060625030426
42337CB00018B/3200